DISCOVER YOUR WAY TO

MAKING IT

Find your creative process
and forge your own path

Create what brings you joy.

First edition

ISBN: 978-0-6458502-0-8

To everyone with dreams.

Preface

Improving our skills in any craft requires self-teaching. Although there is an abundance of information available to us, it is through practice and experimentation that we gain the most knowledge. No one can teach us this; it is solely up to us to be willing to go through the process and make our own discoveries. Creativity is a skill we can all develop over time, and it plays a crucial role in our discovery and personal growth.

As I wrote this book, I reflected on my personal journey and the process of learning and improving in different areas of my life. Through repetition, I have learned that trying something once gives me the confidence to try again with something new. This repetition has helped me develop my unique creative processes that I can apply to many different things. I am confident that anyone, including you, can do the same. All we need is the courage and willingness to start, try, and not give up as we forge ahead.

The primary goal of this book is to aid you in becoming the driving force behind your own personal growth. You have the potential for greatness and the skills to forge your own path. The stories in this book will help you embrace your unique journey and find your own creative processes.

I hope this book inspires you. Through the stories of individuals at various stages of their journey, we can understand that progress and mastery require patience and practice. You can use their experiences as a source of guidance to make your own discoveries.

- Jess

Gratitude and Thanks

Thank you to everyone who let me get to know a part of your life enough to share it as a story in this book. Your stories light the way for others.

Thank you, Universe, for your enigmatic and captivating beauty and the guidance you provide beyond our perception.

Lastly, thank you to everyone participating in my evolution and personal expansion. I am grateful to have had help when I needed it the most.

Contents

Chapter 1

Everyone is Creative

Connect to the creativity that has always been a part of you

Aspire and play

Feeling good motivates us, and we desire to feel good. From athletes to chefs, anyone who has started a craft and then persisted has done so because of how it made them feel. Feeling good is our ultimate "unfair advantage," and it's a prerequisite for being creative and for a desire to hatch.

Desire ignites the motivation to become better, and when we combine it with creativity, we can begin to pave a path.

Desire is our inner fire. It gets us out of bed daily as we continue to shimmy toward our dreams. It's the key ingredient for how we build ourselves brick by brick. Desire gives us energy, gets us excited, and allows us to dream of a better future for ourselves. It is the engine within us.

Our passion for something can ebb and flow; some days, we feel it, and others do not. Desire is unwavering and abundant.

We've all felt what it's like when desire is absent. Maybe you have a job or area of study that isn't fulfilling or doesn't "spark joy." Not all are fortunate enough to "do what we love" at first go, for a living and in life. But the unpleasant grind of doing things without desire is distinct and easy to spot. Instead of feeling inspired and giving us energy, it consumes us, as if freezing us in the steps we were taking toward our hopes and dreams. Getting better at anything requires effort. Luckily, the process is cyclical and straightforward. It doesn't need to end because we can adapt and tweak what suits us as we evolve and grow.

We don't get good at something without effort, but action is more effortless when motivated. This simple guiding principle applies to all our work and our chosen relationships.

Aspiring to be better is a daily affair like a fashion designer who obsesses over a button on a sleeve cuff—and the author researching relatable stories to communicate an idea with clarity. Aspiring to improve is woven into our thinking and the world we create.

The creative process is personal and contextual.

Creativity is for everyone; it has always been within us, even on days we forget. We live within systems where creativity is not prioritized or encouraged. And we were not made aware that being creative is possible for each of us; we don't always consider that creative processes are for us. Yet, we place special groups of people accessing them on the highest pedestals. Has anyone observed this contradiction? It is our choice to be creative (and it is a process). We can awaken the creativity inside of us whenever we want. Use it wherever we deem fit, and invest in ourselves for as long as possible. Our imagination is our workshop, and there are no limits to what we can imagine. We can use imagination to visualize what we want to do or create. As our vision becomes apparent through this thinking process, we can bring our vision to life using desire and a creative process.

The catch is that we only get somewhere if we try. Everyone can imagine, envision, and, by extension, create. When we act on our ideas, we learn; and create an opportunity to practice creativity. Through these steps, our confidence builds.

Informing and shaping this process is our environment and the experiences we gather. It's a simple concept that is unique when in use. Each of us is a unique combination of our experiences, knowledge, and skills. These traits make us different and allow us to offer the world a distinctive point of view.

> *One of the biggest misconceptions of our time is that you're not allowed to create or produce anything until you're good at it.*

The creative process is personal, and it's also contextual. Even though we grow to understand and be masters of what we need for our own processes, we also need other people. Other people help us learn about ourselves and bring various perspectives to consider. Even though your creative process is your own, we share parallels. We combine our individual creative output with other people's creativity and expertise. We all have an "inward" process that works with our "outward" approach. These creative activities that nudge our ideas forward help make us better little by little and day by day. And this is all fueled by our desire to feel good. Approach your aspiration with joy, flirt with your hobbies, and harness creative currency through doing. Through the creative process and the act of creating, we accumulate more skills and confidence we need to continue. Creating is the best way to tailor our processes, hone our creativity, and move us toward our wants and dreams.

Bea

Bea conducted a handful of interviews each day for a research project. Each interview varied in complexity. Booking attendees was a continuous and daily affair for three weeks—scheduling, traveling, conversing, and documenting collected information required much energy. Bea knew she needed to stay focused and nimble to be present and ask the right questions. To do this, she devised a simple strategy to create the space she needed to be creative. Bea left home early to sit by herself at a cafe near work. She spent this time reading and getting to know the people she would speak with for that day. Being prepared made the task manageable, and because of this quick ritual, Bea was clear-headed and creative. It was easy to identify interesting information that came up in the chats in real-time.

This small tweak to Bea's morning routine allowed her to listen intently. Knowing who she was talking to let her explore the conversations more freely. This resulted in a relaxed atmosphere and a safe space for sharing. Insights were revealed naturally through dialogue, which helped Bea identify when her task was complete. She identified and prioritized her needs and took better care of herself, resulting in a better outcome.

This is a creative process at work, as a mentality, strategic approach, and way of living. If we look for it, we will find creativity in our day-to-day lives in small and many ways. Take the act of choosing a new walking route as opposed to your usual path. It heightens awareness of your surroundings and gets you out of "automation mode." How often do we prepare, cook, or eat the same meals? Think of a simple bowl of oatmeal. Get excited by the joy of endless possible combinations by mixing up three different ingredients.

Seek experiences to grow

Once we acknowledge that the creative force lies within, it becomes about persevering on our paths. The courage to try and continue practicing and the determination to show up on days we're unsure. Simply put, we must commit to the process and put in the time. At first, our creative processes may not look like what we imagine. Ultimately the best ways are the ones that work for you.

A hat maker might make many wonky hats along the way, but that's part of their personal, tailored journey of growth. We may feel tentative and face internal and external resistance when we get started. We may want to be better at everything all at once, but we must be realistic about our experiences, growth, and time required. Perseverance and consistency in effort through practice help us develop our natural talents. Some may focus on one area of interest as we improve, while others take a generalist route.

Our perseverance is the path.

We will feel the gap between who we are now and where we want to be. As we go along the journey of continuously improving ourselves, our determination becomes essential to closing this gap. We share a common attraction to opportunities for growth through people, places, and new experiences along the way.

Chapter 2

Take Advantage of Feeling Good

Find motivation by appreciating the joy

Our emotions matter

Understanding what motivates people is essential. It's the first step to unleashing our personal creativity. To understand what motivates people, we must start with ourselves.

Motivation is the outcome of desire, which is easiest tapped into when we feel good. Put another way, when you do things that make you feel good, you feel joy and motivation.

Do you ever notice that when you feel good, your work seems to take on a life of its own? The answers we need appear with less effort; creativity has no bounds and feels "easy"...we have a spring in our step. When we're in a place of joy, this emotion flows through everything we do and say.

Feeling good means being self-aware of our inner
emotional state and noticing when and how we

experience joy.

This concept works in reverse too. Some people consume things that squash their mental, physical, and emotional state. The contrast of identifying things that don't make us feel good allows us to understand better what does. And when we know what makes us feel good, we can use this information to let ourselves be in a state where we can go in the right direction.

We must become familiar with what brings us joy and understand and acknowledge the link between this feeling and our ability to be creative.

What makes us feel good is personal and different for everyone—playing a sport, preparing a meal, socializing with friends—walking your dog, swimming in the ocean, or listening to music. Or, working on your car or painting, the possibilities are endless.

> *Identifying what feels good is an entryway to finding what we love to do and motivates us to do the work.*

Aaron

Aaron is a software developer. Using machine learning, where artificial intelligence helps compute information, he built an app that translates Braille to voice. Blind children do schoolwork in Braille. When teachers review the work, they translate it from Braille to voice using Aaron's app. The app allows teachers to read and grade students' work. Blind children can better connect with sighted children and teachers. Parents of blind children are grateful for Aaron's app. The positive impression it leaves on people makes Aaron feel joyful and motivated.

The tools we use matter

We use specific tools to make a job or task easier. Any device or method that decreases a task's effort creates a good feeling when using it. We might not notice this feeling unless there is a contrast with a more challenging way of doing something. Can you imagine opening a can with a spoon instead of a can opener?

In Aaron's Braille to voice app: teachers use it because it allows them to read schoolwork done in Braille. Blind children use it to do their work and be active class and community members. Their communication process in the classroom is better with the app than without it. As a result, all who use the app as a tool feel included and more joyful. The feel-good cycle created by the app as a tool is a classic "win-win" scenario.

In this scenario, everyone uses the same tool to improve their lives. Teachers, students, and parents go through a process together. They feel joy on an individual level and collectively experience significant benefits.

When we look for things in our own lives that give us that joyful feeling, we can use them to our advantage. To help us in our lives in a small way each day. A bundle of little but feel-good moments improves our lives considerably. When we're aware of this idea, we can intentionally include them in our lives each day.

Chapter 3

Continuous Small Wins

Progress through small victories

Spot the everyday successes

Using feeling good as a guide, we can get ourselves into a state where we are motivated. Recognizing this approach as an advantage to how we operate in the world puts us in an excellent position to begin to notice and build upon our more minor accomplishments. Sometimes motivation happens in bursts, but we can regularly stay motivated by celebrating our small wins.

When we progress at work or on a creative endeavor that matters to us, even if it's small, it's a "small win." When these achievements happen regularly, we find ourselves in a continuous momentum state.

Small wins happen daily, but you must be on the lookout for them; they're not always obvious. We tend to focus on and celebrate big successes. Like getting into University, a promotion, a new job, or a championship. But the small wins keep us going, engaged, and moving forward each day. Big wins are more infrequent, whereas small wins often happen. If you look for them, you can spot small wins daily.

Being present in the moment allows us to connect with those around us and spot the small wins.

Jesse

Jesse loves coffee so much that she wanted to recreate the perfect cup of barista coffee in her own home. Jesse made her first coffee with her new espresso machine with much excitement and high expectations. This first cup was a complete failure! She went through a whole bag of beans without one good cup. Bewildered and thinking it would be easier, she pressed on. Her disappointment settled and expanded into spotting an opportunity to learn. The perfect coffee depended on getting a few things right, such as the grind amount and coarseness and the amount of pressure placed on the grinds before extracting the espresso. She needed to get each part right for a good cup. Jesse adjusted the machine settings each day and noted how the coffee turned out. And each day, she would tweak the settings, getting one step closer to the perfect cup. After a couple of weeks of trying and another bag of coffee beans, she finally made the cup of coffee she was after.

Her persistence and willingness to build on each small win throughout the two weeks led to success. In her case, each day allowed her to improve her coffee-making skills.

Positive emotions provide the motivation we need to continue as we inch closer to our goals.

While Jesse's example is only a cup of coffee, the idea of small wins applies to anything we undertake. A continuous small win sparks joy and motivation. These wins help us persevere and chip away at our work while feeling good. Feeling this way makes us more creative and the process more enjoyable. Just like being present can help us spot small wins, we can use the same presence to spot what actions help us create small wins. It's different for everybody.

Lauren

Cooking is an activity that Lauren has always loved to do. She grew up in a cooking family, and her mother was an excellent cook. Lauren discovered that she also enjoyed cooking and jumped at the chance to prepare meals for loved ones. When someone eats something you crafted with care, it's easy to be present! Reactions are almost always immediate and visible. It was these reactions that Lauren noticed. The audible "mmm" as someone rolled their head back and closed their eyes. The gasp of excitement from a delicious or unexpected flavor. Lauren's small wins were her family's momentary displays of delight.

Lauren's family's reactions are her small wins and excited her to cook, time and time again.

> *"My family's reactions brought me right back into the kitchen to keep creating."*

Lauren carried this idea into her career and training. She persisted in becoming a better and eventually professional chef.

In the beginning, we followed our natural talents toward what felt right. We used this feeling to discover what we wanted to do or create and what mattered to us. We know that feeling now and follow it to spot small wins every day. While not every experience brings us joy and purpose, knowing what to look for helps us land in or find the right place. We discover meaning and happiness by progressing on something that matters to us.

We use feel-good feelings to find, discover, and acknowledge what works.

Feeling like we have meaning in life makes life more enjoyable. What feels like a sense of meaning and purpose is different for everyone. Some find meaning through the work they do or the family they create. If the environment means a lot to you, working on environmental issues may bring meaning to your life. If you want to help people in physical pain or suffering, helping people heal or become strong might bring meaning and happiness.

For homemakers, the love of their family and the act of supporting their children provides purpose and makes life worthwhile.

A sense of meaning and purpose helps us feel whole and content even in the face of challenges. We learn that we can design our lives to achieve the outcomes we seek as we arrive at this place. We can find, do, and create work that is fulfilling.

Chapter 4

Become Better by Focusing on Specific Parts

Pinpointing parts of your unique process

Improve by recognizing what to focus on first

Imagine being at the store, determined to find the most delicious melon using traditional methods. We perform many steps in the intricate process of choosing the best-tasting melon without seeing or tasting it. We search for a symmetrical fruit that is firm and free of bruises. We lift it to gauge its weight, seeking a heavy melon that fits its size. Occasionally, we gently tap it as we've heard that a ripe melon makes a hollow sound. Although we're unsure why, our fingers instinctively dance across the melon.

The steps that make up this elaborate guessing game are creative parts of a process designed to help us figure out the best pick. When we break it down, we derive the details of this process from facts, which help us assess and make determinations. For example, we look for a heavy melon as it is a sign that it is ripe and full of juice. Similarly, the design of scoring processes in examinations helps gauge where we stand and whether we are suitable for the opportunity ahead.

Identifying component parts

It may sound simple, but identifying the individual parts of a process can sometimes be a puzzle. We can reference and gain tips from our predecessors for puzzles others have completed before. What about situations where we are either the first to experience? Or when we don't know anyone who can guide us?

We can develop ways of seeking and obtaining the information we need. We can look at distinct parts of our methods to better understand what to focus on, where we should start, and what we may need.

Many people desire to be "better," but defining better is more demanding than knowing you want to improve. Improving is a process that takes time. It is impossible to improve at anything overnight; we are a constant work in progress. Our expanding values shaped by experiences unique to our life are as colorful as our personalities. It is at this point that being specific helps us move along. Setting an intention to make an improved version of ourselves is the first step in identifying weaker component parts. This action helps us figure out where to focus our improvement efforts.

Rebecca

Rebecca, a Junior Experience Designer, was applying for jobs and was not hearing back from companies. She figured she did not stand out enough. So, she started focusing on getting attention by creating videos and hand-written letters. Rebecca was more skilled in research than in visual design. Still, she was applying for jobs that required visual design skills. Rebecca was, though, very adept at communicating research through hand-sketched storyboards. She realized that attention might not be the right way to promote herself. Getting attention wouldn't help Rebecca if she weren't a good match for the job based on her skills and strengths. It wasn't so much about getting attention as it was about better framing and communicating the skills she already had. As well as improving the skills she needed for the job she was seeking.

> *Going through a job search made Rebecca realize the parts she needed to focus on to get the future job she wanted.*

The work we do demands different skills and tools. These skills and tools may change as we advance. It's unrealistic to expect to be good at everything, but having awareness of the different component parts of your work can help you figure out where to focus now.

How identifying these parts helps us get better

We can understand the component parts of our methods by being more attentive. We can draw a map and design our approach by breaking down the pieces that make the whole. By pinpointing what we enjoy most or areas we are naturally talented in, it becomes clear which parts need more attention, especially those skills that support our strengths. Understanding that it helps us to remain flexible as our plan might need updating as we go.

To become better, we need to understand the individual parts that make up our whole.

There are many aspects to being a good athlete. In a basketball player's case, talent comprises components like dribbling, shooting, and passing. If we break those component parts down even further as part of shooting, there are free throws, three-point shots, and jump shots. A basketball player may select a different aspect of their game to improve at any time. They may decide to work on their free throw to make them a better, well-rounded player. They spend the next few weeks focused on this component, even if no specific situation calls for it. This type of concentrated improvement is also called dedication.

Sustaining long-term betterment of ourselves calls us to identify where we should focus our efforts. Being aware of our abilities and improving where needed helps us become better for ourselves and others.

To continue expanding and growing, we can think about the direction we want to go and the parts needed to get there. Then we can determine what to improve upon and when to continue on our path. Improving and reaching our goals is a process, and it takes time. We can use continuous small wins to build on our previous progress and stay excited. By acknowledging successes, we can maintain the motivation and momentum that helps us move forward each day.

Brett

Brett joined his company as their first Designer. He slowly then quickly became the face of design for the company. A few years ago, Brett started hiring more designers and managing a small team. It became clear that juggling the different management and job responsibilities would be tricky. Brett was having trouble organizing and prioritizing his tasks. Knowing that no one around him could help, Brett set out to find a mentor to help guide him.

> *To become better, we need to understand the individual parts that make up our whole.*

Pinpointing component parts helps you become better

Recognizing the components that are part of our processes, work, or situations takes some thought. Once we see the picture more clearly, we can gauge how much effort to put in. As a result, we'll be ready to progress and feel less overwhelmed. It is here that we can better design our lives and our futures.

> *An excellent place to start is to pick a specific area (a process, a scenario, a challenge). Ask yourself if you can identify the parts that positively affect the outcome when improved.*

Think of a work or life situation where there is tension; it is not going as smoothly as it needs to. What and which part doesn't feel good? Why is there friction, ambiguity, or discomfort in the unknown? What details can you improve upon by yourself, and where might you need help from the outside or someone else?

All the knowledge we accumulate will lead us to bigger, more fruitful wins in the future.

When we have an approach to getting better, we can figure out what to do next, like plucking an apple from a tree. Using this system helps illuminate our path and direction and sets us up for a series of continuous small wins. Sure, we'll experience some failures along the way. Even when—especially when—we stumble, we learn. The improvement of ourselves and the creative processes we use to design our lives assist in our successes, small or large.

Chapter 5

Getting Good

Leverage our natural talents to build and grow

Improve by doing more of what makes you happy

It takes time to reach our goals; we are a continuous work in progress. We can speed up the process by identifying what parts of ourselves to focus on and build upon first. For many of us, this works best by focusing on something that we're already good at and enjoy. Our natural talents allow us to dive in with some confidence and allow us the chance to build on what we already love and feel good about doing. We can use this positive energy as momentum to keep moving. And when we start working on aspects that we're not so good at or enjoy, our previous progress and experience will help us get through it. When we come up against challenges in our process, they are easier to overcome because our past and recent successes encourage us.

Max

Max is an avid motorcycle rider. He got injured riding off-road and started building bikes while he was recovering as a way of passing the time. He didn't have prior experience building bikes but loved to ride and was passionate about making things. Max took his talent for creating and focused on building custom, one-of-a-kind bikes. He made and sold two bikes using a "learn as you go" process and getting better through trial and error. Motivated by this success, he decided to advance his hobby further and start a business. Max has been making custom bikes now for a handful of years. He never creates the same bike twice; each build is unique. When starting, Max didn't have all the necessary skills or knowledge. But he focused on his passion for bikes and his love for building. He got started and experimented as he went. Combining his love of bikes and his love for building helped him move and grow, which kept him inspired and motivated to learn the rest, bit by bit.

We are the designers of our lives.

Improvement isn't always for the sole purpose of creating a career you love. Sometimes we improve for personal reasons and as a way of making our own lives better. By extension, when we become aware of a process of improvement that works best for us, we can apply it to anything in our lives.

Once we achieve something we set out to, we begin to understand that we can do it repeatedly. Once we have some experience under our Beat, we don't need to start from scratch. Learning from these experiences, we can build our very own frameworks. We create templates from our experiences and the creative processes we develop along the way. Within these templates are the techniques and ways of working and living. These templates change and evolve; we can use them to quicken reaching our goals time and time again. They become part of us.

> *We are the designer of our lives, and we can develop processes that help us meet and build upon our basic needs, creating fulfilling, healthy lives that allow us to thrive.*

Suppose our body is our machine; we can optimize our engine through personal expansion by design and intention. A healthy body runs smoothly, allowing us the energy to work on our hobbies and professional aspirations.

> *Often, we cannot focus on bigger goals if our machines are not operating well; thus, it's important to design our lives for healthy living.*

Rachel

Rachel has two hobbies she's been improving upon for as long as she can remember. They have been with her for her whole life because of the joy they bring. These hobbies make her feel happy and balanced, adding enjoyment and value to her life.

Rachel has been writing and cooking since she was young. She views writing and cooking similarly concerning the creative process; she feels joy from putting words together. She feels the same way when putting ingredients together: she gets excited to see and taste the outcome.

"In both cases, I relish the process of creativity. The discipline it takes for things to come out the way I hope they will, and the satisfaction from creating something that people like."

Rachel started writing as a child. She continued practicing and improving her skills throughout college, writing stories for classes and national Websites. She now uses writing as a tool to share her passions and knowledge with others on her self-published blog.

Rachel enjoys the solitary, reflective time that writing provides. This feeling becomes amplified when she shares it with others. She has even taught her partner how to cook!

"Cooking is therapy for me! It feels good to fill my body with the good stuff."

Now they make dinner together a few nights a week. This ritual allows them to spend quality time together while going through a creative process she loves.

What makes us happy is personal.

We all use tools to help us complete a task. A barista uses coffee beans, a weighing scale, a grinder to get the right amount, different kinds of milk, and a coffee machine. A designer uses pen and paper to sketch. And a digital design tool to create the designs on the computer and their storytelling talent to communicate them.

The tools of your craft are your own. They are different

for everyone, just as the parts needed for your process are your very own.

It's not to say that our tools must be unique; you need to find what works for you. And even when we use similar tools as others, we each have our personal strengths, which is a tool in and of itself for creating a unique experience.

Sarah

Sarah, a barista, makes coffee as good as anyone and uses similar tools. One of her skills is building relationships with people like suppliers and distributors. She makes people feel valued through genuine interest in them, sharing her passion for coffee, and asking questions. Others discover that they want to open up to her and help. Sarah looked for the "perfect in her eyes" decaffeinated coffee bean. She was after a bean with the traits she loved, closely matching the caffeinated beans she uses. While sharing the story of her search with one of her suppliers, the supplier recalled a decaf bean he had recently sampled.

The supplier got hold of a sample for Sarah, and after testing it, she loved it. This exchange would not have happened if Sarah did not share her desire for the perfect decaf coffee bean.

She created an authentic connection and a stronger relationship with her supplier, and so he was happy to help her.

We cannot copy and paste someone else's tools or processes

into our template and expect it to work. It's tempting to look at another's success and replicate the same outcome for ourselves using the same tools and steps. Perhaps we try it as a way of learning or experimenting, which is always OK. It is important to tap into our own inner power, authenticity, and individual perspectives to create something unique and personal for ourselves. Pay attention to your own feelings and understanding to determine what works best for you. Often, we cannot focus on bigger goals if our machines are not operating well; thus, it's important to design our lives for healthy living.

Only we have the power to manifest our unique creations.

Have more fun

We must explore and try different things to find what we are naturally good at and what makes us feel positive emotions. We rarely get everything right the first time, and as much as we don't want to hear it, work is involved. If positive emotions followed us around all the time, everyone would be happy!

We can envision building upon those positive emotions to achieve more when we notice what feels good. Have more fun! Fun and play are fuel for our creativity. We're more open to new ideas and other perspectives when we're having a good time. We experience less resistance and are brimming with excitement at the possibilities. We see the merit in other people's opinions and want to build on them.

The less resistance we hold onto, the more absorbed we become in discovery and curiosity, which become driving forces.

Pinpoint ways to take your natural talent or hobby and have fun while exploring and practicing your skill. Start creating and making. Familiarize yourself with different aspects of your skills, including the tools you need. Come to understand what you need to get better. It's OK to start small, and in fact, it is the best way to start. You don't want to take on more than you can handle and feel discouraged before even beginning. Be a sponge, and become the navigator of your destiny through the quest for knowledge.

Chapter 6

Continue, and Practice Through Experimentation

Play, experiment, and have fun

Learn through practice

It's exciting to begin a journey, even though it may feel daunting. There is so much to learn! It can feel overwhelming and out of reach as we focus on the gap between where we are and where we want to be. However, if we look at this from another angle, it's an exciting time of growth as we stretch ourselves beyond what we already know. The journey to getting good takes time; when we focus on improving one thing at a time, we get good faster. Even though we can achieve many things in our lifetime, learning and growing in the most effective way possible makes sense.

In this time of expansion, growth lies ahead of us, and we can expect some level of discomfort. We grow and expand by applying our creative processes to opportunities and experiments, some of which we create independently. We use these experiences as opportunities to explore, find, learn, and improve ourselves.

An essential requirement of this process is finding or creating opportunities to improve our skills and, most importantly, to have fun while we are at it.

Experimentation allows us to practice and learn through play and trial and error. This process allows room for unplanned "happy accidents" and experiences that would not otherwise happen if the path ahead included all the steps neatly drawn out. Happy accidents are opportunities for our growth and expansion. They shine a light on our work in areas we might not have thought about or known are where our natural talent lies. We never know when experiences will be stepping stones to something more significant, but we will never come across these happy finds if we are not open to them in the first place. Make room for trial and error, and never underestimate the power of play! We don't need explicit permission to try something new; we do it if we choose to. Sometimes experiments work out; even when they don't, we can expand inside and out when we are determined enough.

Jess (Author)

I spent several years freelancing as a digital designer in New York City. At one point in my life, I became more focused on writing. One day an old friend, interested in freelancing for the first time, emailed me asking for advice. I thought about all of the different bits of feedback I could share and thought it made sense to take this as an opportunity to experiment and write an article about it instead of answering my friend directly.

I used my friend's help during the writing process to make sure my article answered all her questions; it turned into a small guide to freelancing.

This article about freelancing became one of my most-read pieces. I created an opportunity to practice and experiment by combining my love of writing with a desire to help and teach. I used my writing skills and turned my response to a question into a guide for everyone to use.

When we "play" and experiment, we don't necessarily have to show our work to anyone; it can be just for us or as a means of practicing. We can choose to practice in private or in public. By practicing in public, we create the opportunity for feedback. Whether it's what we consider "good" or not, feedback helps us improve through critical thinking. We won't always feel ready to show our work to others, but growing and expanding sometimes requires us to get outside our comfort zone.

Grow and thrive with determination

Once we identify our vision and the parts that make up our process and craft, we can get specific and select which areas to improve and in which order. By focusing on particular components that support our innate talents, we improve as a whole efficiently. We get joy from doing what we are naturally good at, and by starting with our natural skills, we have the strength to work on the parts that do not come as naturally or easily. We must be patient, which is most challenging when just starting. It might feel frustrating, but frustration is determination in disguise. We'll begin to have faith in our abilities when we see ourselves improve.

We may recognize a gap between where we are and where we want to be when we begin. This recognition is normal and takes time, but we get good and close this gap with time, practice, and determination. We can shimmy through challenging times while holding onto the knowledge that what we desire is possible.

Brian

Brian began his profession as a software developer; he got into the field because he wanted to build applications. Brian is a technology enthusiast and enjoyed reading about technological innovations growing up. He found the technical side of app development intellectually exciting but not personally fulfilling. Brian explored the design aspect of app creation as part of his journey. He wanted to grow in this part of the development process, focusing on how people interact with apps and, therefore, influence the apps' design. Brian shifted his focus to becoming an app designer and described the early stages of exploring design as a distinct gap between his taste and design skills. He was determined to improve over time and with practice. Brian has a passion for technology and yearned to improve our experience interacting with apps through design. As Brian began designing apps, he studied the differences between the apps he loved and the ones he created. He identified areas for bettering his skills and working towards the caliber of design of those he admired.

The motivation to become a better designer encouraged him to improve his skills and continue collecting learnings from his projects with a clear intention of bettering the next one.

Often, we view all unknowns as risks we are unwilling to take. We can't plan everything, and we might not know how our efforts will turn out, but when we explore with an open mind and curiosity, we are sure to be pleasantly surprised by what we learn about ourselves. Despite the discomfort of exploring unfamiliar spaces, we expand and move towards an improved version of ourselves when we intend to have fun. By creating a path for ourselves that includes what we are passionate about and love with what we desire and want, we experience more joy and "happy accidents" while doing the work that helps us improve over time.

Chapter 7

Forge Ahead With Confidence and Courage

Move toward your vision

Bring your dreams into reality

Becoming better at something by focusing on what we're already good at and what makes us feel good allows us to build the foundation to work on the bits that don't come as quickly or easily. Using natural talent as a starting point gives us the encouragement and energy to work on the parts that we feel are more challenging. With this confidence, we are ready to attend to other parts of ourselves that need our dedicated care and lift ourselves up continuously and efficiently.

You might be surprised; getting better at any one thing may not be as hard as we initially thought. And if it is, be motivated, knowing that getting better at everything is merely a process that takes time.

Frustration might arise again, but it often comes from being unable to see things happen when or as fast as we want. Having explored ways that work best for us, we see that anything is possible because we have been through this journey once or twice. You know that getting good at any chosen part is just a matter of perseverance and time. Once we are comfortable and familiar with the steps that work for our learning needs, we can create our own way and guide; we can use this template for anything.

Tash

Tash dreamt of being a filmmaker; specifically, she wanted to direct a film. Scared to start, but with the support of friends, she made a short film about her favorite spots in her neighborhood. She wasn't interested in the filming and editing aspects, but getting started meant she had to be willing to sacrifice; to engage with parts of the process, she didn't necessarily want to do. Energized by her desire to direct, Tash wrote a script and put together the visual plan of shots. She guided a friend with a drone to capture the story she planned. She shared her simple film, with beautiful imagery of scenic Australia, on social media and received much praise. Next, Tash improved her scriptwriting skills by taking a class and making another film on the back of this success. Bettering this skill meant she could produce a short movie and experience all the steps this time. With her newly acquired skills, consistent practice, and perseverance in the process, she entered a local film competition and won an award. Tash's determination to direct films helped her navigate and design a creative process she made just for her. Despite skill limitations initially and difficulty getting the right equipment, Tash achieved her goals by starting small and growing over time.

Tash created her path; experimenting and learning along the way, filling in her knowledge gaps allowed her to make movies and share her work with a larger audience.

Her approach is remarkable on its own. For anyone at the start of an exploring stage, sharing our creative outcomes or any part of the process can be scary! We always learn and make progress in some shape or form.

Occasionally, we find ourselves stuck and may ask others for assistance. It helps to be aware of all the different parts, what we need help with, and when it makes sense to ask for guidance.

Know your strengths and when to ask for help

It is easier to progress when we start with aspects of our work that come naturally. And when we start expanding from our positive attributes, the whole process becomes a bit faster and more comfortable, and we can achieve "flow." Flow is an automatic state; we act or create without thinking too hard. It's enjoyable, and creativity, even at work, can take on a life of its own in this flow state.

Pay attention to your emotions and how you feel throughout this process. You will notice when enough aspects of your process begin to work, and you feel like it clicks and comes together easily. You will feel better and more able to balance the discomfort between the known and unknown, including what we thought we thought we could not do before. This accomplishment is exciting as we recognize within ourselves that anything is possible! We can then make progress a bit quicker than before and take on any problems that may come our way.

Phin & Phebes Ice Cream

At one stage in my life, my partner at the time and I started an ice cream company. We made delicious ice cream at home that we wanted to share with the world. We loved the process of coming up with surprising yet approachable natural flavor combinations. Before going into business, we took the opportunity to educate ourselves by going to Ice Cream University; yes, there is such a thing! There was still one area in which we didn't feel confident when we graduated. That was coming up with the recipe for our ice cream base. Ice cream is food science. We didn't know what would work best when a pint of ice cream had to go through various modes of transport and sit on a shelf in a grocery store for weeks at a time. Recognizing we needed help with this task, we hired a food scientist to help us with our formula. Getting help meant we could continue preparing other parts of our homemade flavors for stores. We learned about our strengths and experience and developed a profitable food product.

We may be able to learn and complete most aspects of our process independently. Even so, it feels daunting at first trying to match our vision with our expectations as we can't be good at everything immediately. Tash could have worked with an editor, but she was the one who best understood her vision. Determined to execute the story with minimal compromises, Tash pressed ahead. Later in her career, she might focus only on directing and working with a professional editor. This time around, she decided to learn and master all the parts needed for her betterment and personal experience.

When we wanted to make our ice cream available to more people, the complexity of creating an ice cream base formula delayed our vision of bringing delicious, natural ice cream to the masses. Getting help enabled us to be attentive to the other parts we needed to move along, including the fun bits like coming up with more flavor ideas.

These stories show different ways to reach goals.

In both stories, there was a determination to overcome difficulties and learn what was needed. This exercise may mean recognizing when we need help from people with more experience to move us ahead. When we begin or face the unknown, we feel resistance, knowing there is a distance between where we are and where we want to go. This distance stops many people from trying new things or even starting.

Over time, going through and repeating a learning pattern, we become mindful that expanding our knowledge can feel uneasy. Nonetheless, we become more aware that the discomfort is temporary. We grow more confident each time we go through this. Even when we have this experience only once, we learn how to use our methods of creating to overcome challenges; break down barriers bit by bit through determination, effort, and persistence.

As we go through life collecting our small wins, we bring our creative processes with us. They are the templates that we can improve on and use to bring our vision to life. We may be unaware we have these, as it is not a skill we consciously acknowledge. But we use a template each time we do something. We use different parts of our unique processes, learnings collected from various experiences. These become part of your body of knowledge, designed for you.

You are deciding and creating who you want to become. The basketball player that spent time improving their free throws might apply similar steps when learning a new language. The foundation you have built up to this point will become a launchpad for bigger, better things.

Chapter 8

Build With Others to Improve Ourselves

Nurture, explore, and create

Work with others to rise

Throughout life and in our careers, we continuously progress as we cycle through the path of discovery and, later on, improvement. When we start in our own environment initially, it is just us, with the support of guardians from time to time. We experiment, play, and create to explore what we enjoy and discover what we are good at. As time passes, we improve the skills we learn and feel more comfortable within ourselves; this increase in confidence lets us be our best, share our work, and team up with others' talents. It feels a little daunting yet exciting when we collaborate with others. Our talent is riveting when combined with a partner or group because we multiply our strengths. When faced with any complications, we are informed and encouraged beyond the limits of our knowledge and ideas. A new kind of confidence embraces us. One that comes from being part of a team and witnessing the value of your talent and contribution move a task toward completion, even if in ways that may seem small at first.

We learn through experiences, some of which we gravitate towards, others we create. When we are in a team, especially with skilled and talented people, we learn from them and each other. Although we, not our teammates, are responsible for our transformation, we evolve and grow with their presence and support. Our expansion speeds up when we work with others, discovering more about ourselves, our capabilities, and our new talents.

The area we choose to get better at has a different purpose. Now that we better understand the direction we are moving in, we can decide which projects and people align with our vision. As we continue playing, exploring, and practicing, we move past multiple learning phases and progress toward our vision. Play allows us to explore freely, to gain fundamental skills for building our distinctive foundation. Practice helps us put the skills we cultivate over time to use.

Refining our natural abilities means recognizing where we can contribute and being more deliberate in making progress toward our vision through our daily choices.

We do this many times in our life. Considering it this way, we know that getting better takes time; it is a non-linear process composed of many experiences. Imagine many pieces of fabric strung together, each representing a piece of knowledge learned and collected from our experiences. Each one we gather and add to our existing selection makes for a unique cloth that gets wider and used in more ways as it grows.

Persevering and practicing is an ongoing discovery. Sometimes we do it alone; in most cases, we are with others, learning with and from each other. When we explore and expand, we create opportunities to adjust, hone, and pick the most suitable device in our creative tool kit in the way it is most effective for us. And when we are functioning at our best, we have more fun and are more open to absorbing knowledge from happy discoveries along the way.

Going through a discovery process with other people can feel challenging. We can't plan or anticipate what might happen. However, we can get excited that this process presents unique conditions for creating. It creates a setting for talents to be combined to witness our effort in making a shared vision happen.

We can focus on our contribution when we create with others who share their unique gifts as part of a process done together. When we combine our unique talents with people with special skills, we can focus on developing our area of specialization. Once you understand how to have the most impact, you can take on your next endeavor.

Zoe

Zoe has played the piano for a couple of years. Until now, Zoe has spent most of her time playing alone, on occasion, in front of small crowds. Zoe was invited to perform at a jazz festival with a group of musicians. The group consisted of ten professional musicians playing various instruments. This experience allowed Zoe to practice her talent in a new environment, take her skills, and co-create. Zoe is comfortable with her expertise but had never played with such a large band. How would her ability contribute to the group's performance with ten other specialists? Would she be confident playing on a piano provided by the venue? This performance and the support of a professional team allowed Zoe to face perceived limits courageously. Zoe walked off the stage with the experience of what it feels like to play as a professional. Now, she comprehended that what she desired existed and was attainable.

We get better each time we observe evidence of progress. Encounters like Zoe's, are opportunities for us to see others who have achieved a similar vision. We may not want the exact result, but these experiences may help us recognize the adjustments we need to make to move in a specific direction.

Through each experience and learning from people along the way, we gain confidence for our next steps. This accrued knowledge enables us to work through adjustments, bringing us closer to our vision even if the change is small.

As we gain experiences, we decide how to broaden our knowledge and who we surround ourselves with within the process.

Laurel

Laurel became interested in photography at a young age. Following what felt natural, Laurel enjoyed photography as a hobby during high school. She refined her composition skills through college while studying visual anthropology. Visual anthropology explores how we share our culture through images, such as film and photography.

Eventually, Laurel continued photographing as a professional. During this time, she partnered with a writer to create a photojournalism book in the United States. Laurel's photographs recorded the lesbian, gay, bisexual, transgender, and queer interviewed, a production that respectfully documents their diverse lives.

Laurel combined her passion and talent for photography with her desire to contribute images to anthropology. These images formed the visual aspect of the community she interviewed, providing an authentic platform for the LGBT community to share their stories.

As we move through different stages of our development, we adjust our creative methods. We develop efficient ways to recognize how we use existing ones—especially when working with others.

Stay determined by recognizing your accomplishments

We often refer to past learnings to determine what may be suitable in a current setting; it might be so subtle that we don't even notice. Our reflection lets us know when our efforts to improve, along with our continuous practice and combined experiences, start to harmonize.

When we are present and not merely showing up, self-expansion is assured. We find that we can accomplish what we set out to achieve. This realization gives us the determination to progress, the physical energy, the mental strength, and the ability to persevere through any difficulty.

Our unique combination of talents and experiences is where we start building.

This awareness helps us see where we're at compared to where we want to go. With this knowledge, we can embrace what we discover about our desires.

Our vision of the future has no limitations. There was a time when telephones were not wireless, and mobile technology was an idea far from possible. We could not have imagined our reality now in the past, and we learn that it took many iterations and wild ideas for us to get to where we are today. It did not discourage us from our vision of a wireless way of connecting, nor should how we get to our vision dissuade us from taking steps toward it. When we work to uncover what we are truly capable of, we create who we are becoming. Adjustments along the way help us be prepared and glide through the unexpected. As an outcome of our effort, we will see that we are useful even in small ways.

Chapter 9

Perseverance is the Path

Show up and step into your future

Persistence lives within

We may find it easier to stay excited about things around us that seem to be changing or new. The process of learning, discovering, and creating often offers novelties. It feels like this at the beginning of a journey and when we encounter growth and expansion. Akin to how everything a baby sees, and experiences is new and awe-inspiring.

When absorbed in newness and this type of excitement, motivation flows. When we don't feel motivated, we may be tempted to look for it outside ourselves. Although this tactic might seem natural, if we do not choose what excites and encourages us, we risk being at the mercy of conditions out of our control. When our source of motivation comes from within, and our actions are for the good of us, we find the strength and consistency we need. Our results are meaningful and swift. If we look to external sources for consistent motivation, our actions may not align with what is suitable for us, and moving in the right direction is more challenging. We may stop altogether.

Nonetheless, the kind of motivation that lives within will constantly stimulate us. Each action we take towards our goal feels good, and it's as though we can't control the urge to act! It is reassuring when our motivation flows from within. Our days feel effortless, and we are more or less delighted to be chipping away at our daily tasks.

> *We can feel the impact of motivation when it's present and even more so when absent.*

There will be days—or periods—when we don't feel motivated. A lack of motivation does not mean our vision is not relevant anymore or that passion does not exist. When we care about what we are working towards and understand where we are going, the clarity we gain over time will reveal what we need to make our dreams come true. We will have moments where we don't feel motivated enough to continue during the process. At times, we won't feel good enough—and that's OK; it is a sign that somewhere inside, we recognize the gap between where we are and where we desire to be. The outcome we create from here depends on how we act and respond to this feeling. Undoubtedly, it is more challenging to show up when it seems we don't have an option. In particular, we don't want to turn up in environments with resistance. There will be occasional uncomfortable clashes when working with others, but we will work through it bit by bit when we show up.

We must remember our vision along the way, what we

envisioned, and our desire. Imagine desire like the place you grew up but no longer live. It's always with you. Especially when exhausted and you recognize there are challenges ahead.

When we don't necessarily feel up to it or ready, showing up requires staying persistent. Exploring our path requires us to persevere through the challenges. We can use the small wins we achieve and the difficulties we overcome along the way to keep us motivated.

Setting out to get good at something or do bigger things than we've done before is hard. Not giving up when it is hard to figure out answers to difficulties creates room to be more creative.

For some, persevering can mean learning new skills or getting better at those we already have. For others, it means getting better at the other areas that support their talent. When we focus, we progress at our strengths before getting good at complementary aspects. This process gives us more confidence and clarity. A cook who wants to become a chef may cut many bags of carrots to improve their knife skills. Perseverance means repeating this many times until reaching a certain level of confidence and skill level. The resulting orange fingers are proof of endurance. An experienced cook takes these steps to realize their dream of becoming a chef.

Patience is a must, as progress takes time. Self-awareness is a tool for recognizing what is valuable and noticing potential in the discoveries you stumble upon along the way.

Karina Seljak, Seljak Brand

Karina's interest in textiles, and waste-less approaches, began during her time in Queensland, Australia, studying Fashion Design. She was always looking at materials for inspiration; comprehending their finite nature made her realize the large amount of waste involved in clothing production.

She understood that waste is not solvable by one well-designed product alone. Karina set out to research different production processes and ways of consuming things. As she continued her exploration and analysis, Karina partnered with her sister, who has sustainable project management skills. Together they focused on local resources and became inspired by wool.

Australia, where the sisters live, produces some of the best wool globally. Australia has a history of making hard-wearing blankets passed down from generation to generation.

The idea of making blankets was appealing as people from all walks of life used them. They spark positive emotions. People become emotionally connected to blankets as they signify warmth, comfort, and safety. It is a product loved by people.

The sisters shared a passion for the planet. Using this as motivation; they found an environmentally friendly, sustainable, and profitable model. They eventually founded Seljak Brand and started to make quality wool blankets.

The pair started by communicating their shared fundamental values. They also acknowledged their respective areas of interest and strengths. Karina found a way to manufacture a product from recycled and renewable resources. Her sister, Sam, continued expanding on their connection with the community in ways that were ethical and mutually beneficial. A portion of proceeds from blankets sold go to the Asylum Seeker Resource Centre (ASRC) in Melbourne.

The Seljak sisters leaned on each other's strengths and shared a desire to further their knowledge in their individual areas of expertise.

> *Sharing a dream of a future without waste, they envisioned creating a product that would not harm the planet—all while supporting a social mission.even more so when absent.*

After one of their blankets has enjoyed a useful life, they collect it free of charge using a carbon-neutral courier service. Back at the mills they work with, they shred it and spin it into new yarn to make future blankets. This closed-loop model allows the company to divert waste from landfills and continuously create blankets of value.

By sharing their story, they inspired many with the help of press coverage.

Through their research, the Sisters chanced upon an alternative model and discovered the circular economy. In a closed-loop approach, this model designed to benefit the environment, society, and businesses matched their fundamental values. This model was an exciting find. It puts the planet first and reduces waste to almost nothing while allowing the Sisters to make a product people love.

Instead of starting afresh, the sisters focused on their unique skills and looked directly around them for tools and resources. Prompted by the impact of waste in manufacturing, they explored sustainability. In time and with an open mind, they persevered to develop their expertise to create their own path and a unique product.

As a result of the sisters' determination and accomplishment, Seljak Brand has made hundreds of people open and aware of a reality that opposes what we think we know is possible. More businesses now know a better alternative to creating products that generate positive outcomes from all perspectives.

> *"It's fascinating to watch other businesses and even industries emerge over time, and to be part of it." — Karina Seljak*

Staying true and determined

We can all make use of perseverance. This type of endurance can take you places you never thought you could go—your very own uncharted territory.

Although there are other factors to making progress, perseverance means we are consistent in our efforts; as we gather our small wins, progress begins to compound like a train that slowly, then suddenly picks up speed.

> *Watch perceived limitations fade away as you carve out your way and achieve the "impossible." Even though there are no overnight successes, you can still win every day.*

Perseverance is most useful when we have a goal we're passionate about and determined to achieve. It's paired best with a quest or a mission! Determination plus perseverance allows us to deliver on what we set out to do. These traits are best together, like peanut butter and jelly. Together, they give us the drive we need to move forward and continue doing so regularly.

Chapter 10

Make Your Luck

Open new pathways using your intention

Initiate the right opportunities

Have you ever thought about how we consider someone lucky?
Is it because they always seem to meet the right people? Do
opportunities appear at the right time? Is it just a matter of luck,
or is it something else?

The ability to chip away at and work toward something—to
persevere only works if you've identified your vision or goal. We
tend to think of dreams or ideas as having an end state. Once
we get there, though, we continue to persevere and have
conviction in doing what is necessary to keep our end goal in
motion. Making it to the big leagues is a dream for many
professional athletes, but a new journey begins once there. At
their core is conviction, and professional athletes must continue
training to be at their best for the game.

Even when we take a different route to reach our goals,

our drive comes from the initial vision; it is at the core.

Our decision to do or become something creates an intention; we carry a desire to reach a specific outcome with us. Determined to realize our vision, we make small steps toward it. Our intention fuels our determination to realize our dreams and watch them come to life.

People often say that there are many chapters in a lifetime. That is another way of saying that we can do and become many different things in our lifetime. We can upgrade our vision of who we are through what we discover. By reaching a goal once, we can see that it is possible to do it repeatedly. Once we set our sights on something, our intention leads the way, and we can achieve it through concentration and determination.

Our path is lit by a beacon of light when we combine a vision with desire, determination, and intention.

Alara

Determined to find a career she enjoyed, Alara started thinking of other options and paths. She worked in Marketing for technology companies and learned a lot but was ready to expand her knowledge into other areas. She felt prepared for a new adventure. Looking into the future, Alara could not imagine being happy in her current role or industry. Alara knew lots of happy software developers. Curious if she might find a similar position enjoyable, she decided to give it a go. She left her job and began exploring the journey of learning how to code. Coding aligned with her desire to work in a constantly evolving field and includes an element of change. She could upgrade and learn something new all the time if she wished.

Learning to code was tough. Even experienced developers face challenges in solving problems and coming up with solutions.

Alara discovered a way of approaching problems and applied this template to coding. As a professional developer, Alara views coding as "calm problem-solving." This approach helped her persevere through her learning trials and stay focused on her desire to work in an ever-changing area. Often, developers will hit a dead end when coding; if there is a bug or something is not working as expected. This experience occurred almost daily when Alara was learning this new skill.

> *She always kept two things in mind, a belief there is a solution and an imperative to stay calm during the process.*

This approach to "calm problem-solving" enabled Alara to stay focused when she learned how to code. Determined to explore the possibilities of this career path entirely, she trained her thinking to look at the "problems" she was faced with and moved calmly.

Using this approach, she takes on each challenge, one at a time, on her journey to becoming an experienced developer in a career she enjoys.

There was one more thing, though. After learning to code, Alara still needed to put her skills to work and begin her career as a developer! She decided to intern and landed an internship at a software company. Determined to create her new career path, she worked hard and focused on specific coding values essential to the company. After the 6-month internship, the company offered her a full-time role.

Alara set her sights on a goal and set out to make it a reality. Fear of the unknown, impatience, and frustration are all things we encounter on our journey to getting good. Faced with challenges, Alara or anyone going through a similar experience can decide not to continue. But like Alara, anyone can remember their determination and work through the challenges. Sometimes we try things, and we find that they're not suitable for us, and that's OK too.

Alara's hard work and effort opened doors that led to her breakthrough in coding and new career beginnings. It's not so much that the opportunity came to Alara; it's more that she created the opportunity.

What we call luck is actually preparation paired with opportunity.

Jess (Author)

I once worked at an education company as a designer of the company's software to help tutors and students have learning sessions online. A customer service team member approached me with a dire request one day. This team ensures customers have a good experience with the product. The customer service team used an outdated software platform, making it difficult and time-consuming to complete everyday tasks. As the company grew, the frustration the team experienced only got bigger. The customer service team asked for my help; they wanted me to redesign the software to do their jobs better. The team's level and quality of service impacted the company's bottom line. I already had a job looking after and designing the company's flagship product. But I wanted to help and had a particular passion for redesigning hard-to-use software.

I knew I could work on one project without it impacting the other.

I floated the idea to my boss at the time. Concerned that it would take too much time and focus away from my primary job, he asked me not to do extra work. I knew I could make it work, and I was determined to help the customer service team; I proceeded anyway. Working against the clock only made me more determined. I designed a streamlined process to engage the team and design the new software while getting the best input from everyone around me. Since the group was so excited about the project, they prioritized it and gave me the time to get feedback to push it forward quickly. The redesign came together in a few short weeks and was successful. The team burst with excitement in reaction to seeing the final product. The company saw a marked improvement in key metrics, and the customer service team was much happier with the new platform.

I could have strolled along, saying no to the project, especially as my boss advised against taking it on. But I knew I could make it work. Motivated by my passion for redesigning software and determination to make a difference, I made it work. This excitement and the help and feedback from others helped me redesign the platform in record time. And the company improved because a critical team had a better tool to do their work.

It is incredible what we can achieve when we are determined.

It may never be "easy" to reach our goals, but setting an intention is a powerful force that helps propel us; it's a starting point. When we set our sights on something we are passionate about, our determination helps us overcome blockers and challenges. Determined to help the customer service team, I devised a plan appropriate for the context and timing. And Alara persevered through a process of internal expansion to create the pathway to her new career.

We can plan to the best of our abilities and knowledge, but we never know how the path will unfold ahead of us. Motivation helps us get through it. No matter what happens along the way, we can adapt and course-correct. When facing unexpected obstacles, we may feel disappointed momentarily, but when we are clear about what motivates us and determined to continue, we'll find a way. With each experience, we grow to appreciate all parts of the process.

Chapter 11

Powerful, Sprightly Teams

Use each other's strengths and unique points of view

Move forward together

There will come a time when we get paired with others or need to navigate a better way within a group. When we pursue our own goals and pick who we work with, we aim to partner with people who are a good fit for us. When we get placed into a group and don't know the personalities and how best to highlight everyone's strengths, we need to pause thinking and feel our way around. Getting to know people better is always needed to work out how to surface effective dynamics.

Going through this experience can feel surprising as we learn that not everyone behaves like us or shares similar views. Everyone is different and brings their own life experience into the mix, like a giant quilt where each patch that makes the quilt is distinct.

When we work within a group, we want to create an

environment that helps us move forward as one.

Working within a group allows us to explore and achieve things we wouldn't be able to do independently. When things are working well, we may push ourselves further than we thought possible for the team's sake. If we choose to focus on our differences in perspectives in situations like this, we're likely to experience friction and resistance. This dynamic slows us down and creates less-than-satisfactory results for everyone involved.

Instead of embracing collective diversity and strengths, teams concentrating on how painful it is to work with one another will find creativity hard to come by. People in a group like this will feel a general sense of glumness.

Ideas flow, flourish, and come to life effortlessly when we work together effectively.

Imagine a scenario where 20 dancers attempt to dance to the same music simultaneously. Each team member has some ideas about what might suit the theme best. However, as a team, more focus is required to narrow down which ideas work best. If the dancers had to shout their thoughts to convey them, no one would hear anyone else. Instead, should the dancers quickly vote on everyone's ideas and select the one they feel most compelled to develop, that would be the starting point of a cohesive vision. Turning the concept into a concrete vision, the selected dancer could work with the music composer to identify or work out the parallels in their themes to create the structure of their desired outcome. Bringing their vision and individual talents together, they might decide to involve another dancer who has been with the dance company for an extended period and understands each dancer's performance strength. Together, they bounce ideas around, do quick experiments, and refine the vision in the process. They lean on each other's strengths, highlight each dancer's talents, and continue choreographing the piece together.

The outcomes of this pairing, which continuously improves itself, are the same as the process we have covered in previous chapters. In this way, we can say our approach to developing ourselves benefits the entirety of the team. This small team produced a collection of scenes that made for fantastic choreography. The group at large got excited at being part of the process and their progress, creating a common goal and motivation for everyone.

A small win for the group is a win for everyone.

Imagine another scenario where one comedian attempts to draft a comedy sketch. Starting with a blank piece of paper, the author thinks through different ideas, unsure if they would be funny to a live audience. It takes the comedian longer to produce the first draft alone than if they had a few people to work with who also understood their vision. Paring up with others to brainstorm or get feedback can speed things up.

It's not to say that we can't produce incredible results alone. However, as we take on increasingly ambitious projects, it makes sense to pair up with others. Working together, we help each other expand our perspectives, get better results, and achieve more significant outcomes than we could with our knowledge alone.

Sometimes it is a matter of finding our "people." These are people we enjoy being around and thus work well with for many reasons. When we are around people we feel safe with, we are comfortable and transparent and share our ideas, feelings, and processes. We feel like we can express our most authentic selves, encouraging one another to do the same, somewhat "accidentally," and creating an environment where we embrace everyone's experiences, perspectives, and strengths. Including a broad range of perspectives brings about diversity in thinking, which helps us be more creative. We can better envision an ideal future and see our vision come to life because the answers to problems we're solving reveal themselves to us much more effortlessly.

Creativity thrives in functional groups and allows the path that unfolds to do so with ease and feel evident and seamless.

Use all your senses to make choices

Who we surround ourselves with is important; the people around us impact us even though we might not see it. We come across others with different opinions, colorful personalities, adding to our life experiences. It does not mean we are aligned or share similar values, nor should we expect that from anyone. However, we know that those who celebrate our wins are the ones who support and encourage us through the peaks and troughs of our expansion process. No matter how small, the people who witness our successes hold us accountable and enable us to move through challenging experiences.

Not everyone around you will understand what a small win looks like, and not everyone appreciates the value of momentum or is interested in your growth. Some people are happy to witness your process, and some will want to play a part as a collaborator or active motivators, encouraging us to explore outside our comfort zones. Others wish to experience wins, but only for themselves. It is perfectly normal to have various friends and family in our lives. It's important to make wise decisions and be aware of the people we spend time with. If surrounded by those who prioritize their own interests, we should reflect on our choices and how they may impact our lives. Through self-reflection, we may discover that we are acting selfishly, prompting us to reconsider our actions and the kind of person we want to be.

> *We know what an empowering experience feels like when we team up with the "right" people.*

We communicate our thoughts and ideas, feel respected, and can return the favor to find a happy place where our joint talents shine. Nevertheless, crafting effective ways to contribute as a unique individual in a group setting is never straightforward, as the talent differs according to the pairing in each scene. We know for sure that finding a balance that works benefits all involved; the best of both worlds leads to rewarding outcomes. Knowing this concept means we can be more aware of what works and when.

Wherever we go, we have plenty of opportunities to be creative and find out how to collaborate better in our lifetime. When we acknowledge our strengths and observe what works and what does not, we can apply the creative process we designed for ourselves to anything.

> *We don't have to wait for others to create a setting that works for us. We can be the ones to observe each other's strengths and, where necessary, suggest alternative ways of working together.*

Jess (Author)

The simple idea of bringing people of diverse backgrounds together to brainstorm is an excellent example of working creatively. Any group of people can sit around a table and talk, which rarely produces surprising outcomes, but it is the most common approach. I facilitate activities that enable people to work together to contribute ideas in a "structured" manner. These activities make the creative process transparent and inclusive. The design and structure are customized based on the needs of the group and the desired outcomes. Activities such as this create a space for focused participation in a fair and open environment, which is crucial.

I use one such approach for teams developing new ideas and features in their software product. This workshop is structured around time-based rounds of sketching. This approach encourages people to think of their ideas as quickly as possible without applying judgment right away. Attendees naturally come up with ideas derived from their particular points of view and expertise. Through a process that facilitates a convergent outcome, in the end, the group comes together on one or two big ideas that combine the group's vision and most sensible logic.

Through the process, people share and discuss ideas that work well and bring them into their individual sketches, integrating and remixing them.

In a workshop like this, people do not know what to expect as an outcome, but they are excited by the structured activities guiding them to try a new way of working. This type of collaboration brings people together, creating a setting based on unity and trust, making people feel more open to each other while working and contributing in a new way.

Workshops like this feel empowering and fun, enabling participants to share a creative process.

The common observation from these workshops is the team's growing excitement from the small wins along the way: creating momentum and the ability to move forward and make change together. Through a shared creative process, people can realize they have strengths they didn't even know existed. The realization that ideas that matter come from real people, all of us. Exposure to working in a new, collaborative way and coming up with an abundance of ideas in a single session creates a bond within the team. Participating in the activities reminds attendees to trust their strengths and observe others' strengths to develop outcomes that they would not accomplish independently.

When we have people around us, we may expect or wait for

others to create change. Nevertheless, we must recognize that we can positively impact our surroundings regardless of how many people are around us. Take a step back, look at your situation, exercise creativity in your approach, find ways to share with others, better your collective ideas, and make and realize them bit by bit. By using one's specific expertise in a new setting and way, each person uncovers creative ways of working within themselves, contributing to the group.

You can show other people that change is within reach, and it does not have to be complicated. Watch other people uncover their own creative processes that expand and enable discovery, just as you did.

The world becomes a creative challenge once you see that you can include creativity in any process for any challenge or scenario. In this game, your role is to bring creativity into your work, especially in the face of obstacles. When you integrate creativity into your way of thinking, you will wonder why you have not done so all along. You'll surprise and inspire by bringing others along on this journey of experimenting with different ways of working. Involving others in and sharing your creative processes creates a ripple effect that can move mountains and overcome any challenge.

Many people will be content and happy with their experience the way it is. Now that you are thinking about how creativity can be part of your every day, how will you use it?

Chapter 12

Becoming You

Create yourself through the process of creating

Activate the creative force that lives within

The completion of certain steps leads us to a more important place. On a stormy work or school day, perfect for sleeping in, getting out of bed is a win. This act of getting going despite discouraging weather contributes to the bigger picture of starting a productive day. We might not even notice the ripple effect created by this small action.

It's unusual to look at the rituals in our everyday life as a win because we achieve them daily. Fumbling, we get dressed and have breakfast. With our eyes closed, we persevere through brushing our teeth. We build momentum and move into the productive day we envisioned with each of these small wins. One productive day snowballs into another, creating palpable energy that gives us the power to pursue our goals and vision. Each productive day adds fuel to our machine while training our stamina. We use this feeling and a concentrated focus on our vision to stay determined for prolonged periods.

In this space and supportive routine, we consistently feel good, which allows us to be productive and creative. This seemingly "simple" idea is, in effect, a foundation for our vision to sprout and eventually thrive. It is here that we can see our path begin to unfold.

Once our foundation is in place and knowing that progress takes time, we can take steps forward by focusing on our innate abilities. And as our confidence grows, so does our momentum and excitement for continuing. Practice becomes fun, and experimentation becomes second nature.

When we show up daily as our authentic selves, we put ourselves first and set the stage for our creativity to be in motion. It accumulates through our small wins, building momentum beyond our personal growth and expansion. Opportunities begin to reveal themselves to us, and areas we can impact become more evident.

Regardless of the space or phase we find ourselves in, whether in school or at work, we continue to develop our sense of awareness when working with others. The strengths of individuals in a team contribute to an environment that speeds up the expansion of all. In a group dynamic, one might find they are quiet yet verbally communicate the team's outcomes the most succinctly. Yet another might find listening to others comes easiest. Listening allows for acknowledging each team member's strengths with ease. Which in turn helps to communicate the focused goals toward which we work. Both examples are steps taken toward joint progress.

There is no one best path; we are on track when we find ourselves useful no matter where we are.

Our path, or what some might refer to as our destiny, is created as we discover who we are and choose where we want to be. Often our environment has changed so much in that process that what we thought we wanted is irrelevant by the time we get there. While our values will change to make way for a future where we can contribute regardless of our gender and creed, we must continually champion our growth beyond what we understand of our existing capacity.

Take the process of creating music as an example. In the past, a composer knew which instruments they would include. They would then write and produce a score for their composition. However, they wrote their songs before the invention of synthesizers and could not involve electronic sounds in their songs because they did not exist yet. In the future, composers will need to write music for instruments that do not exist today. How can we let what we know exists today decide who we may be in the future?

Would a caterpillar think it cannot grow into a butterfly?

It is impossible to know where and how we can contribute in the future. With the gift of hindsight, older people might have already experienced and know this to be true. Should one find themselves in a similar position described above, the focus would be the love for composing an environment made up of sounds. We would spend hours finessing our craft daily with this awareness while leaning into our natural talents. Every day, we would make conscious choices, such as who we surround ourselves with for support or mentorship, the people who comprise our core team and help and challenge us to innovate from the inside out. Who stays with us through any discomfort in the process.

Have you innovated or excelled in your profession yet feel like you haven't grown on the inside? What are the decisions you make every day that reflect a commitment to your own development? Are the people surrounding you in alignment with your desire?

Going back to basics, what have we been saying yes to in our lives? Do we say yes to choices that align with us and our direction? Can we stay open to possibilities that come our way even when we turn some down? Can we pass by things unsuitable for us and our path, even when ambiguity is present? Can we say yes to what is best for us?

What does it look like to innovate from the inside out? Innovating from within is a breakthrough in the usual way of doing and being.

When we acknowledge the passion that motivates us from within, we move through challenges with a concentration that puts us on a fast track to our objectives. Determined to get closer to our core purpose, we find an endless supply of courage to persist through any discomfort of self-evolution. When something feels good, it simply means it matches our desire, and what we act on is helping us get closer to our inner purpose. Looking at it another way, what does not feel right for you, be it a decision, person, or situation, does not match your reason for being in that moment. It could be that an opportunity came at a "wrong" time, but it does not mean it is "bad." As tricky as it might be to turn down an opportunity or person, you know when to go the other way.

From experiences we accumulate, as individuals and collectively, we know that momentum can push our efforts forward and make the process manageable and even easy. In new situations and groups, there is a bit more to consider. Even though all the parts may not perfectly fit together for momentum to emerge, a certain amount of unity needs to exist to create traction. This type of motion does not just appear; sometimes, it needs a nudge to reveal itself. We can use shared creative processes to develop that nudge, quickly becoming a racing lane.

Using a creative process makes us feel alive. We yearn for more as we pile up our accomplishments and do what we didn't think possible. Through the process of creating, we create and become ourselves.

Our education and environment make us believe that creativity is a gift, a talent granted to a selected few. Having divided the creative process into small, approachable parts helps us debunk the notion of creativity being complex, and we can see that creativity is within us all.

Go, create.

About the Author

Jess is a digital designer passionate about helping others achieve their goals. She has a rich background in design and technology and has been instrumental in creating various innovative projects from the ground up. Jess is a mentor and teacher who loves to experiment and provide practical guidance to others. Her dedication to her work has earned her industry accolades, and she is committed to motivating others in their creative pursuits.

Jess, originally from Maine, currently resides in Sydney, Australia. She continues to explore creativity and technology, committed to empowering others through her mentorship and teaching.